Facts About the Black Bear

By Lisa Strattin

© 2019 Lisa Strattin

FREE BOOK

FREE FOR ALL SUBSCRIBERS

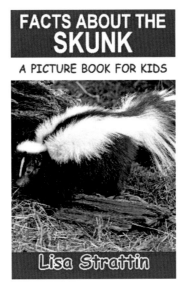

LisaStrattin.com/Subscribe-Here

BOX SET

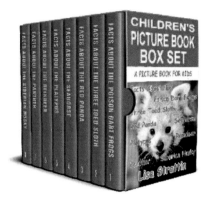

- **FACTS ABOUT THE POISON DART FROGS**
- **FACTS ABOUT THE THREE TOED SLOTH**
  - **FACTS ABOUT THE RED PANDA**
  - **FACTS ABOUT THE SEAHORSE**
  - **FACTS ABOUT THE PLATYPUS**
  - **FACTS ABOUT THE REINDEER**
  - **FACTS ABOUT THE PANTHER**
- **FACTS ABOUT THE SIBERIAN HUSKY**

LisaStrattin.com/BookBundle

Facts for Kids Picture Books by Lisa Strattin

Little Blue Penguin, Vol 92

Chipmunk, Vol 5

Frilled Lizard, Vol 39

Blue and Gold Macaw, Vol 13

Poison Dart Frogs, Vol 50

Blue Tarantula, Vol 115

African Elephants, Vol 8

Amur Leopard, Vol 89

Sabre Tooth Tiger, Vol 167

Baboon, Vol 174

Sign Up for New Release Emails Here

LisaStrattin.com/subscribe-here

Contents

INTRODUCTION

The Black Bear (also known as the American Black Bear) is a medium-sized bear that is found living in a variety of forested habitats all across North America. They are also the most numerous bear species in the world! There is considered to be twice the number of Black Bear animals than all the other bear species added together.

BEHAVIOR

The Black Bear is a mostly a solitary animal and night time hunter. They may occasionally put up with others in their area when a bunch of them gather around a plentiful food source. They spend the majority of their waking hours searching for food in the forest and eat large quantities of plants every day to make sure that they have a good fat reserve for the coming winter.

When the winter conditions set in, they retreat into a den under a hollow tree or in a burrow, where they semi-hibernate through the cold months ahead. They are able to wake up and go out in search of a light snack to break up their long slumber, unlike a true hibernating bear.

Although Black Bears normally move around slowly on all fours on the flat soles of their feet, they are not only able to run at speeds of up to 30mph but when they feel threatened, but they also will stand up on their hind legs to make themselves look even bigger in order to challenge a predator or rival. This posture can lead to aggressive fighting if neither side will back down and retreat.

APPEARANCE

Despite their name, Black Bears can range in color from black to dark red or brown and can even be a lighter tan in certain regions. They have short thick fur covering their heavy body and have a pointed muzzle, small eyes and larger and more pointed ears than their Brown Bear relatives.

They also have shorter legs and claws which makes the Black Bear a much more agile climber than the Brown Bear. In areas where the two live in the same place, they are able to escape danger by digging their claws into a tree trunk and pulling themselves up.

Like all bear species, the Black Bear has an excellent sense of smell which is used to find food and less developed hearing and sight, due to their relatively small ears and eyes.

REPRODUCTION

Male and female Black Bears will briefly come together to mate in the summer then will become solitary again and both will begin to start eating to prepare for winter. After a gestation period that lasts for around 7 months, the female gives birth to between one and five cubs at the end of winter in her den.

These hairless cubs are vulnerable and rely on the warmth created in the den from their mother's body heat to help them to survive the early days. The cubs stay with their mother until they are nearly two years old, learning the skills that they need to survive on their own.

LIFE SPAN

The Black Bear normally lives for 15 to 30 years in the wild.

SIZE

An adult Black Bear can be as tall as 6 feet and weigh close to 600 pounds!

HABITAT

Although the Black Bear is still widespread throughout much of North America, their historical range once covered the forest land over the entire continent. Today they are found from northern Canada, throughout western and parts of eastern USA, and down into northern Mexico. Wherever there is a forest habitat, these incredibly adaptable bears will try their best to survive successfully.

Despite populations in some areas being affected by loss of their natural habitats, the resilience of the Black Bear shows that numbers in most areas are actually increasing as of this writing.

DIET

Although the Black Bear is classed as a carnivore (meat eater), they have a diet that is mostly made up of plants and plant material. Up to 95% of their diet is vegetarian, depending on the food available where they live. They forage for fruits and nuts in the trees and eat grasses, roots and bulbs on the ground. They also supplement their diet with small animals like insects and rodents.

Depending on the region where they live and the prey available, Black Bears are also known to hunt young deer, eat carrion and can also catch fish in rivers (a skill that is particularly used in areas where they don't have to compete with Grizzly Bears for food).

Because they are so large, Black Bears spend most of the night eating, at an average of 12 hours a day, to build up fat reserves for winter.

ENEMIES

Due to the large size of the Black Bear, fully grown adults have few natural predators within their native habitats.

Young cubs are much more vulnerable and are threatened by a number of different predators including: foxes, Birds of Prey and even other grown Black Bears.

SUITABILITY AS PETS

You already know that you would not keep a Black Bear as a pet. If you want to see them and have a local zoo, you can probably visit them in a habitat there.

COLOR ME

COLOR ME

COLOR ME

COLOR ME

COLOR ME

COLOR ME

Please leave me a review here:

LisaStrattin.com/Review-Vol-295

For more Kindle Downloads Visit Lisa Strattin Author Page on Amazon Author Central

amazon.com/author/lisastrattin

To see upcoming titles, visit my website at LisaStrattin.com– most books available on Kindle!

LisaStrattin.com

FREE BOOK

FOR ALL SUBSCRIBERS – SIGN UP NOW

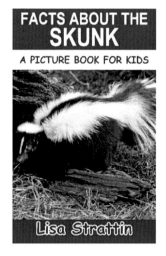

LisaStrattin.com/Subscribe-Here

LisaStrattin.com/Facebook

LisaStrattin.com/Youtube